THE OFFICIAL
LEGO® Harry Potter™
2022 Yearbook

Oh dear, it looks like the Dursleys' house has been taken over by owls. Can you find the owls at the bottom of the page somewhere in this scene?

Harry needs a wand for his first year at Hogwarts.
Use the clues to find it in Mr Ollivander's shop.

Box with
matching lid

✳✳✳

White label

✳✳✳

Two shelves from
the bottom

Has Harry bought everything he will need for Hogwarts?
Enter the numbers of the missing pieces in the
blank squares to complete the scene.

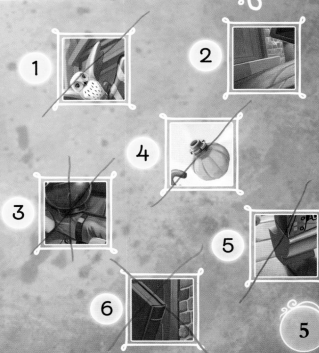

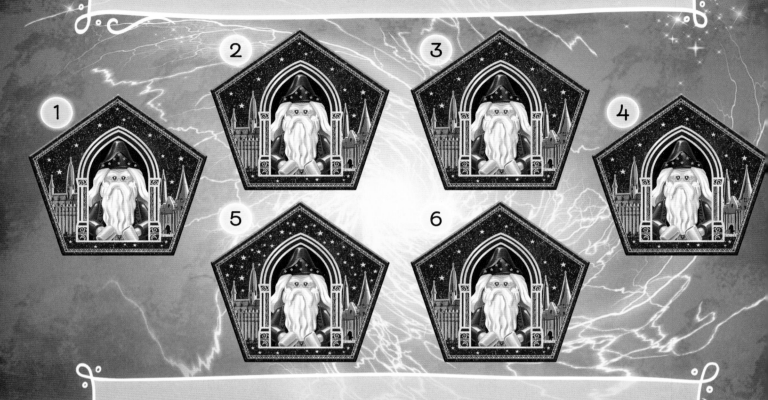

What colour would Scabbers become if Ron's spell works? Look at the sequence of potions below to find out, and then colour in Scabbers to match.

Sunshine, daisies, butter mellow, turn this stupid, fat rat ...

Gryffindor, Slytherin, Ravenclaw or Hufflepuff? Find out which house the Sorting Hat has chosen for these students by counting up the coats of arms and matching the results with each of their plates.

... but where to put you?

After their first meeting at Hogwarts, Harry and Draco knew they would be fierce rivals. Can you find each of the four small close-ups in the bigger picture?

What did Professor McGonagall turn into while she was waiting for latecomers on the first day of Transfiguration class? Find out by drawing around the sequences shown on the left and seeing which animal remains.

What is Seamus Finnigan best at in Potions class?
Making a big BOOM! Can you find ten differences
between these two explosive scenes?

Who is following Harry, Hermione and Ron? A close-up
of the creature is shown in the middle.

Professor McGonagall is an Animagus, meaning she can
turn herself into a particular animal. Connect the dots
to find out which Animagus animal she becomes.

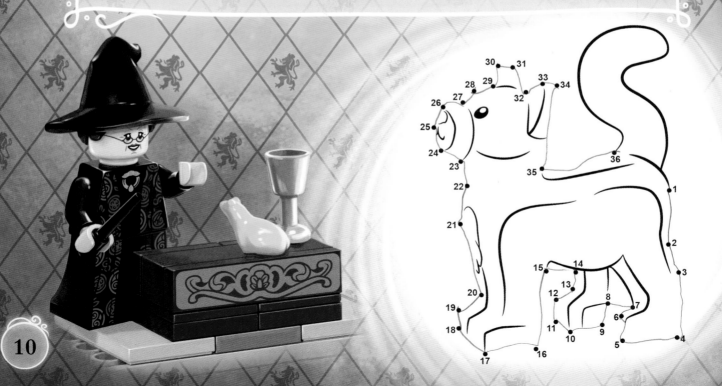

When casting a spell, it is important to use the correct wand movement. Pair up the matching wand movements and the student who is left is the one who will cast a successful spell. One pair has been found for you.

It's hard to find an empty seat in the stands during Quidditch games. Look at the pictures below and circle the fan underneath who is missing from each stand.

1 2 3 4 5 6 7

1 2 3 4 5 6 7

1 2 3 4 5 6 7

1 2 3 4 5 6 7

Harry's broom has been cursed! Using the coordinates provided, cross out the characters in the grid. The one that remains is the wizard who cast the spell.

A1 C2 B1 A2 B2

What has Ron's mum sent him for Christmas? Fill in each section in the same colour as its dot to find out.

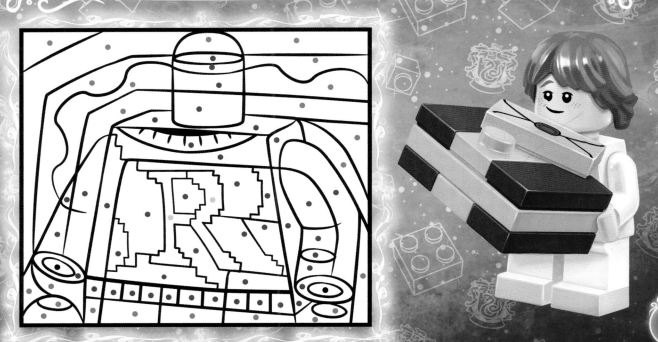

There's no time to lose — Filch knows that someone snuck into the library during the night. Help Harry get out of the Restricted Section by showing him the way through the maze.

FINISH

Who's there? Show yourself!

START

Harry saw a chilling image in the Mirror of Erised.
Discover who was in it by finding the flash that
matches the one on the mirror.

If you go into the Forbidden Forest, you'll need a
guide who will steer you away from dark corners.
Find out who is best for the job by working out who
should fill the empty space in the grid below.

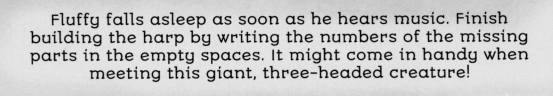

Fluffy falls asleep as soon as he hears music. Finish building the harp by writing the numbers of the missing parts in the empty spaces. It might come in handy when meeting this giant, three-headed creature!

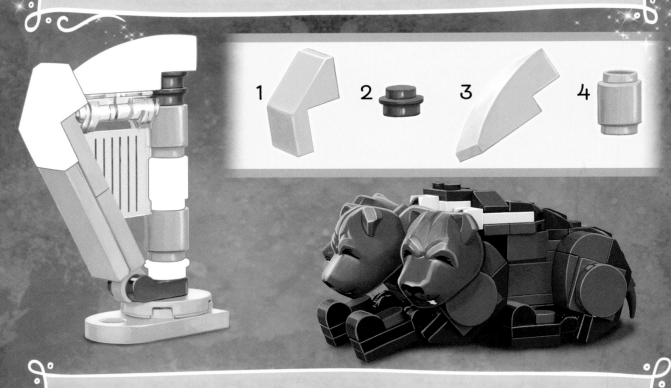

1   2   3   4

Only one of the Flying Keys matches the lock on this magic door. Can you find it? It's the one that's different from the others.

A

B

C

D

E

F

In Wizard Chess, the pieces move by themselves.
Follow the sequence at the bottom of the page to
move across the board from start to finish.
You can't move diagonally.

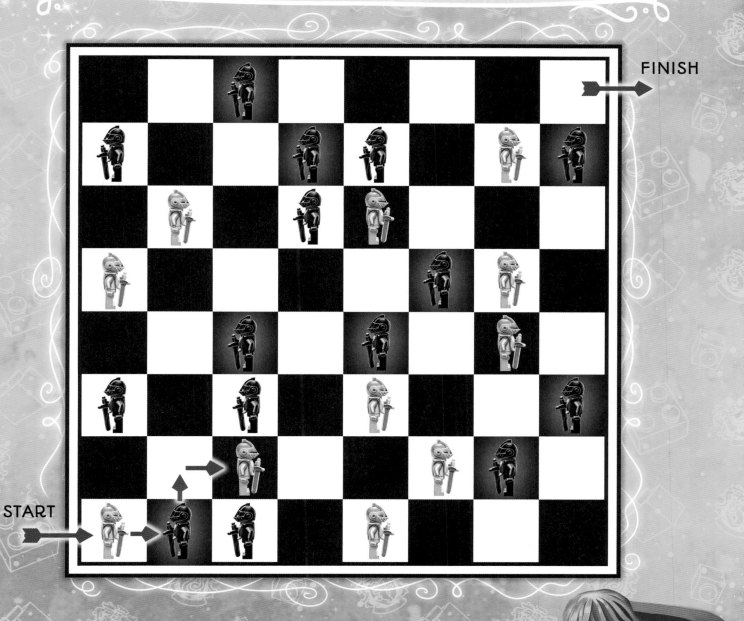

FINISH

START

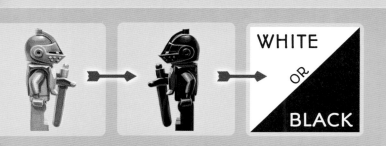

WHITE

OR

BLACK

BOOM! A pudding has exploded in the Dursleys' living room. Match the picture pieces at the bottom of the page to the gaps in the scene, writing the numbers in the correct places.

Dobby is responsible for the mess and is trying to hide from sight. Can you spot him?

A sinister character is lurking in Flourish and Blotts. Find out who it is by working out whose stack of books is identical to Harry's.

A   B   C

After a wild drive that ended on top of the Whomping Willow, the Flying Ford Anglia doesn't look too good! Fix it by using a pen or pencil to draw in the missing parts.

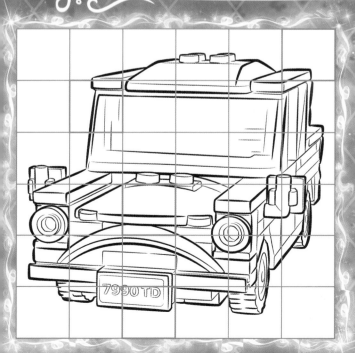

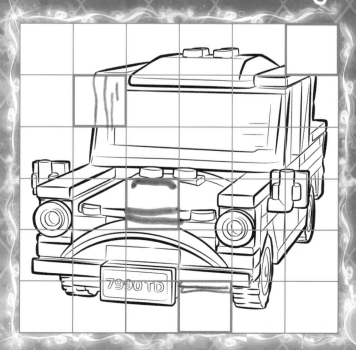

7990 TD   7990 TD

Baby Mandrakes have a deafening scream when you repot them, so you need to do it quickly. Work out the pattern in each row and write the letters of the missing plants on the empty pots.

1

2

3

A   B   C

Who can make Professor Lockhart's portrait look the funniest – you or the Cornish pixies? Grab your colouring pens and pencils and give it a go.

As a punishment, Harry has to reply to all of Professor Lockhart's adoring fans. Number the stacks of replies from the ones with the least letters, to the ones with the most.

Legend has it that one of the Hogwarts founders built the Chamber of Secrets. Who was it? To find out, look at the gallery and find the witch or wizard who looks different in each of their portraits.

The Slytherin team were given new brooms from Lucius Malfoy and now they're unstoppable! Find seven Nimbus 2001 brooms in the Slytherin common room.

Dobby the house-elf always seems to get Harry into trouble. Can you spot which of his shadows is the correct one?

Hello!

Things are getting heated at the Duelling Club meeting. Look at the snapshots and tick 'Y' if they appear in the scene, and 'N' if they don't.

24

What impressive creature did Draco conjure?
Untangle the lines to find out.

Serpensortia!

1

2

3

The password to Professor Dumbledore's office
has a special code. Find the code that matches
Dumbledore's to discover the magic words.

Every Flavour Beans

Chocolate Frogs

Sherbet Lemon

Liquorice Snaps

Harry has cast a spell to make these cupcakes levitate. Discover which charm it was by finding the flash that is identical to the one coming from his wand.

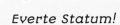

Alohomora!

Everte Statum!

Vera Verto!

Wingardium Leviosa!

Crabbe and Goyle have eaten cupcakes filled with Sleeping Draught. Take a close look at their long nap and find eight differences between the pictures.

Oh dear, Hermione's Polyjuice Potion has turned her into a cat! Follow her recipe to find out what the disastrous concoction looked like.

Recipe:
- Colour the bottles in the order that the coloured drops are falling into them.
- Find the bottle that looks exactly like this one.

Bad news – the Basilisk has taken one of the Hogwarts students. Follow the tips to find out who needs to be saved from the monster's clutches.

The student you seek:

· Has red hair
· Is wearing a black uniform
· Is not covering their eyes

Hogwarts is no place for those afraid of ghosts! Use pens or pencils to fill in each section in the same colour as its dot to reveal the spirit of Moaning Myrtle.

This dark passage leads to the Chamber of Secrets. Help Harry and Ron follow Professor Lockhart into the chamber.

START

It's really quite filthy down here.

FINISH

Dobby is a free elf! He stood up to Lucius Malfoy to protect Harry Potter. Which circle below contains these four poses of the house-elf?

Sirius Black has escaped from Azkaban! Look very closely at the fugitive's poster and find the correct prison sign.

The Knight Bus is unusual because it can change shape to fit through small spaces. Help it get back into shape by labelling the muddled pieces with the correct letters.

Dementors are swarming everywhere! Can you tackle them by grouping three together at a time, with each one in a different pose? The first group has been done for you.

Professor Lupin knows what will help him recover from his encounter with a Dementor. Do you? Test your eyesight and find the treat that only appears once.

Hurry, Divination class has already begun! Help Hermione get to the right classroom by following the stairs and avoiding the obstacles.

FINISH

START

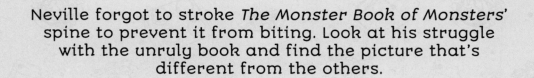

Neville forgot to stroke *The Monster Book of Monsters'* spine to prevent it from biting. Look at his struggle with the unruly book and find the picture that's different from the others.

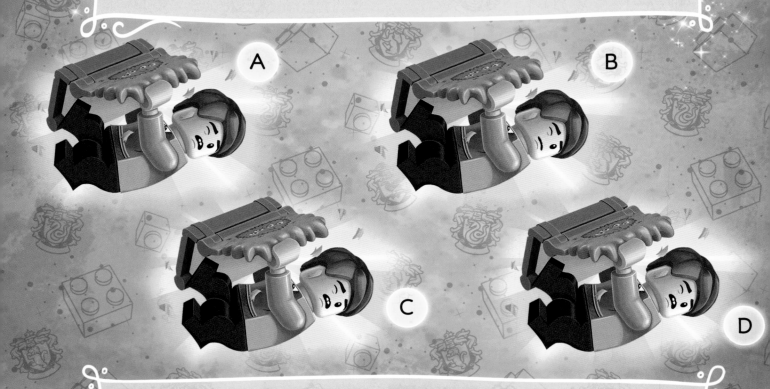

A

B

C

D

Oops, one of the Slytherins made Buckbeak angry! Find out who it was by working out which student is missing.

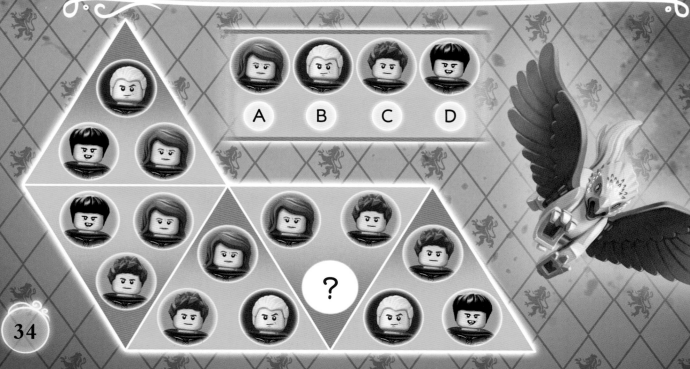

A   B   C   D

The prisoner of Azkaban has escaped and is hiding in Hogwarts. He has just scared off the Fat Lady. Help her return safely to her portrait by writing the number of the correct picture piece in each of the gaps.

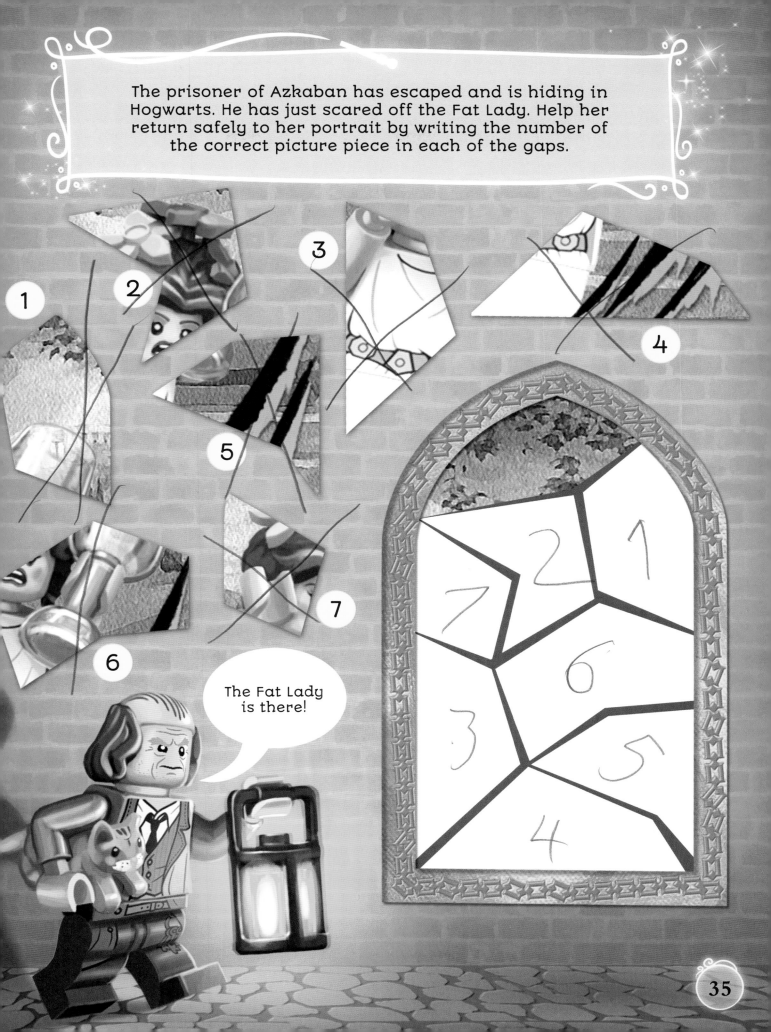

The Fat Lady is there!

With the Marauder's Map, Fred and George can play as many pranks as they want! Practise using it by marking where each of the four squares can be found on it.

I solemnly swear that I am up to no good!

Dementor on the horizon! Quickly connect the dots to conjure your Patronus, so it can protect you from the hooded creature.

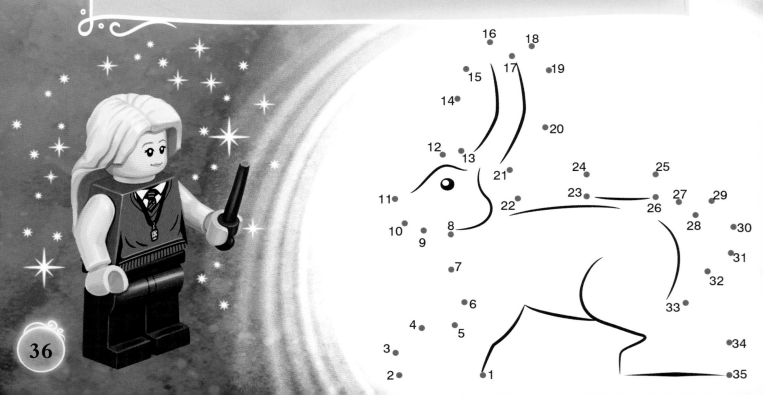

36

Oh dear, Scabbers has run off again! The numbers in the sequences below tell Ron how many squares there are until the next obstacle. Help him catch the rat by choosing the one that avoids all the obstacles.

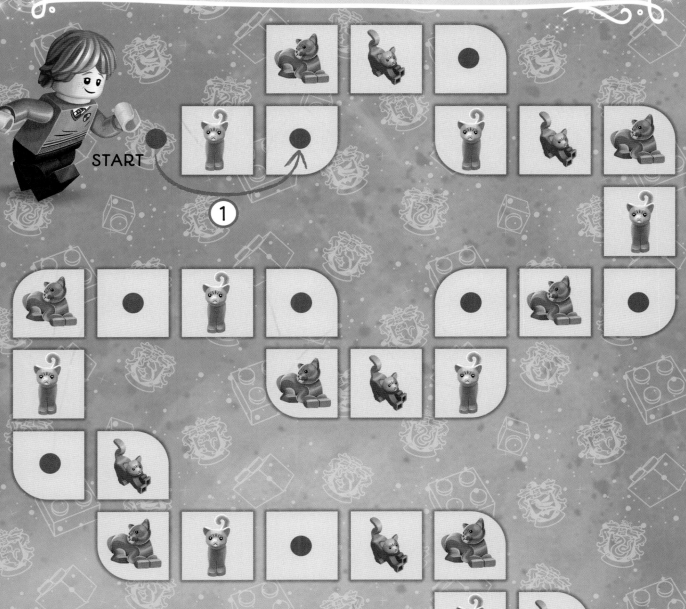

START

1

FINISH

(A) 1 - 2 - 1 - 3 - 4 - 3 - 1 - 3 - 2

(B) 1 - 1 - 1 - 3 - 1 - 3 - 1 - 3 - 4

(C) 1 - 2 - 4 - 3 - 1 - 3 - 1 - 2 - 2

(D) 1 - 2 - 4 - 1 - 3 - 1 - 2 - 3 - 4

37

These are the schools that take part in the
Triwizard Tournament. Untangle the lines to
match the names with the correct crests.

Hogwarts School
of Witchcraft and
Wizardry

Beauxbatons
Academy of Magic

Durmstrang Institute

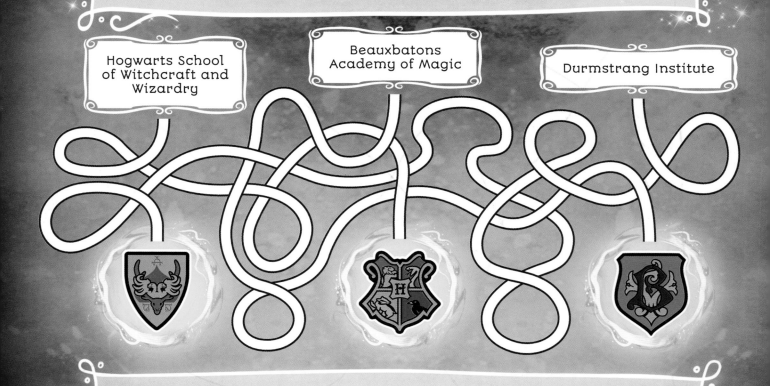

An article about the tournament participants appeared
in the *Daily Prophet*. Take a look at the photo on the front
page and tick the snapshots that appear in it.

Who drank the Ageing Potion? Look for the pair of portraits without matching frames to find out.

Harry needs to get the golden egg, but it's guarded by a Hungarian Horntail. Help him choose the route where the fire-breathing dragon appears the least number of times.

A

B

C

A piercing scream came from the golden egg when Harry opened it! Finish the jigsaw to see the effect it had on its listeners.

Neville is limbering up before the Yule Ball. Work out his sequence of movements and put the correct numbers in the circles to complete the pattern.

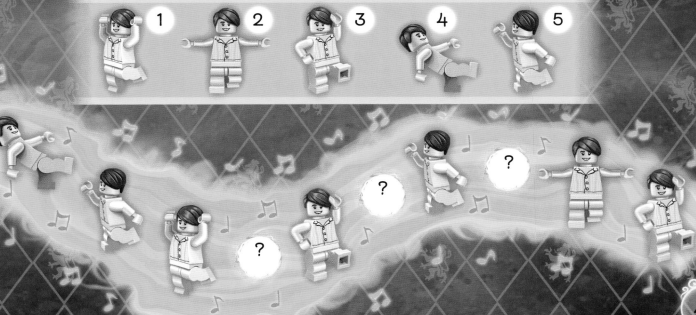

Finding a partner for the Yule Ball is not an easy task. Follow the clues to work out the pairs, and then mark their stars with matching colours.

- floral dress + black bow tie
- dress with dark pink sash + white bow tie
- dress with bow + red shirt
- dress with light pink sash + ruffled shirt

Not everyone can see Thestrals. Reveal this amazing creature by filling in each section in the same colour as its dot.

Thestrals are quite gentle, really.

Point out the portrait of Professor Umbridge that is different from the others.

1

2

3

4

5

Which piece is the missing door to the Room of Requirement?

A B C

A very dangerous witch, Bellatrix Lestrange, has escaped from Azkaban. Join the search by marking the places where three matching portraits appear next to each other. One has been done for you.

Ha ha ha ha!

Oh, no! Dolores Umbridge has taken control of Hogwarts! Can you work out which of these students is one of her favourites? It's the one that doesn't have a magical quill pointing toward them.

Any student in noncompliance will be expelled.

45

Professor Dumbledore is a master of Apparition. This means he can instantly transport himself from place to place. Look closely at each picture and circle the jigsaw piece that will make him disappear.

1

2

3

4

Who do these mysterious silhouettes belong to?
Match them to the right characters.

A   B   C

Luna has lost her trainers. Help her by finding the pair
of shoes that match the ones on Luna's poster.

MISSING

A   B

C   D   E

Professor Umbridge was pestering one of these magical creatures. Untangle the paths to find out which one it was.

A

B

C

D

Number these pictures of Professor Slughorn's magic hourglass from 1 to 5, where 1 has the least fallen sand and 5 has the most.

The sand runs in accordance with the quality of the conversation.

1

Who is Ron's biggest fan? Work out the sequence below and write the numbers of the missing portraits in the empty circles. The character in the red circle is Ron's number one fan!

1
2
3
4
5

It's time for the Battle of the Seven Potters. Discover who took part by finding the portraits whose coloured bottles are in the same order as the ones on the shelf.

Complete the grid so that there are three different people in each row and column. The person who lent their wand to Voldemort will appear in the green square.

I require your wand.

Help Mad-Eye Moody plan the Seven Potters mission by colouring in three more squares where the participants should appear. The squares on either side of the red line need to be a mirror image of each other.

The Order of the Phoenix was formed to protect the Wizarding World from Lord Voldemort and his followers. Connect the matching picture pieces to reveal this secret society.

The power of the Sword of Gryffindor comes in handy in troubled times. Can you surprise Griphook by finding the sword that isn't covered by another?

Only a goblin would recognize that this is the true sword of Gryffindor!

There is one identical character in each of these neighbouring groups. Can you find each one?

Where is Salazar Slytherin's medallion? Follow the colour sequence shown to find out who holds this precious keepsake. The first two lines have been done for you.

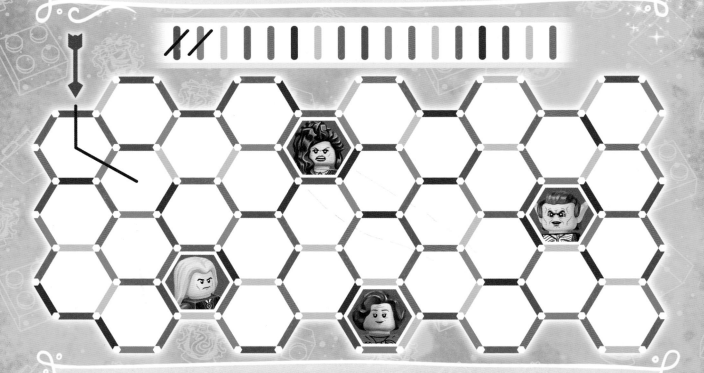

Dobby helped Harry and his friends on a very difficult mission. Follow the instructions and draw a portrait of the brave house-elf.

1

2

3

4

Can you find Lord Voldemort's supporters in the crowd?
Circle the six sets of portraits in the grid.

55

Harry, Ron and Hermione need to get into Bellatrix Lestrange's vault at Gringotts as quickly as possible. Can you show them the right way? Be careful of those sharp turns!

D

START

C

A

B

FINISH

The Weasleys are some of Hogwarts' bravest defenders.
Take a look at this courageous family and write the
number of the hero who is missing from each circle.

What a beautiful memory! Make it clearer by writing the
letters of the missing pieces in the empty squares.

ANSWERS

p. 4

p. 5

p. 6

p. 7

B · A · D · C

p. 8

p. 9

p. 10

p. 11

p. 12

p. 13

p. 14

p. 15

Wingardium Leviosa!

Sherbet Lemon

p. 29

p. 30

4

AZKABAN PRISON ×T1390
AZKABAN PRISON ×T1939
AZKABAN PRISON ×T1930
AZKABAN PRISON ×T1930
AZKABAN PRISON ×T1330
AZKABAN PRISON ×T1303
AZKABAN PRISON ×T1930

p. 31

B E D C A

p. 32

p. 33

p. 34

B

B

p. 35

2 1
7 6
3
4 5

p. 36

DRACO

p. 37

D

p. 38

Hogwarts School of Witchcraft and Wizardry

Beauxbatons Academy of Magic

Durmstrang Institute

p. 39

p. 40

p. 41

1
4
2

p. 42

p. 43

5

How to build Lucius Malfoy